DAD JOKES

TERRIBLY GOOD DAD JOKES

VOLUME 2

Get a FREE eBook!
sharethelovegifts.com/free-offers

1.

**Why should you
never trust atoms?**

*Because they make
up everything.*

2.

**Did I tell you about
my new hedge trimmer?**

*It's cutting hedge
technology.*

3.

**What bird
can play chess?**

*Well, Toucan play
that game.*

4.

**Why did the farmer buy
so many baby chicks?**

*Because they
were cheep.*

5.

**Why did the hen
run away?**

Because it was chicken.

6.

**I'm sure glad I
became a locksmith...**

*It's opened lots of
doors for me.*

7.

I lost my phone in a pear orchard...

It was easy to find, its an Apple

8.

How did the night watchman sleep?

On his side, with an eye mask.

9.

**Did you know hearing
aids are on sale?**

*Their prices
are unheard of!*

10.

**Why was the ship captain
mad at the dog?**

*He kept
disemBarking*

11.

My son doesn't have a visa to get into the United States.

He only has MasterCard.

12.

I ordered a quesadilla...

Just one dilla is fine. A case is too much!

13.

How does a vacuum cleaner work?

It sucks.

14.

Did you hear about the horse in the hospital?

She's in stable condition.

15.

What do you call a house full of dog hair?

A shed.

16.

Mom colored her hair red in the bathroom ...

It looks like someone dyed in there.

17.

**Is the mushroom
a good friend?**

He seems like a fungi.

18.

**I want to store my
portabellos in the fridge...**

*I don't know if there's
mushroom left.*

19.

What happens when you have English after algebra?

English is the aftermath.

20.

What do you call lunch meat on the floor?

Below knee!

21.

Did you hear about the robbery at the Apple store?

There was an iWitness

22.

How do you know when a calligrapher is tired?

Making Z's.

23.

**I got a new
dry erase board.**

It's remarkable!

24.

**How do you find
the diameter of a dessert?**

Use pi.

25.
Did you hear about the candle party?

It was lit!

26.
What did God say when it was time to save the animals from the flood?

"I Noah guy."

27.

**I want to
practice maritime law...**

*Just have to pass
the sandbar first.*

28.

**I've got a lot of coins, but I
don't know their value ...**

I'm not good with change.

29.

**I got fired from
the calendar factory...**

*When I decided to take
a few days off.*

30.

**I heard the cross-eyed teacher
was very forgetful.**

*He couldn't
keep his pupils straight.*

31.

What do you call a white bucket?

Pail.

32.

How do ducks smell?

Fowl.

33.

I thought about making a belt out of watches...

Then I realized it's a waist of time.

34.

How did they fix the pirate's injured eye?

They patched it up.

35.

I dropped my Greek salad on the floor!

Oh well, olive.

36.

The guy at the seafood shop is so greedy.

I'd go as far as to call him shelfish.

37.

**My boy is
very bright...**

*That's why
I call him sun!*

38.

**Why doesn't
dad eat bananas?**

*He doesn't
find them a-peeling.*

39.

What do zombie kids do when their dads embarrass them?

They roll their eyes.

40.

Nineteen & twenty had a race. Who won?

Twenty-One!

41.
How did the
fish plead in court?

Gill-ty.

42.
Why did the cow break
up with her boyfriend?

She needed to moove on.

43.

**I had to throw away
the cheese shredder?**

It was for the grater good.

44.

**Do you know the joke
about a piece of paper?**

Never mind... it's tearable.

45.

Why did the shark seem suspicious?

Because he was fishy.

46.

How do witches verify their hexes?

They use spellcheck.

47.

Where do you go to get small soft drinks?

Minnesota.

48.

Did I tell you about the time I spilled vinegar everywhere?

I was in a pickle!

49.

The first French fries were not actually cooked in France?

They were cooked in Greece.

50.

What is the most musical fish?

Tuna fish.

51.

What happened after the rainbow robbed the bank?

*He went
to prism.*

52.

Why shouldn't you trust an acupuncturist?

*Because he'll
stab you in the back.*

53.

**Why are ducks
bad doctors?**

Because they're all quacks.

54.

**Why should you
not trust dermatologists?**

*They make
rash decisions.*

55.

What do you call it when several fathers exit quickly?

Ske-Daddle!

56.

Why were the hamburgers arguing?

They had a beef.

57.

**How do you get
a boat delivered?**

You ship it.

58.

**Two guys walked into a bar.
What did the third one do?**

Duck!

59.
I sliced my
finger when cutting fruit...

Now we have blood oranges!

60.
Dad,
I'm hungry.

Hi hungry, I'm dad.

61.

You can always store your photos on the cloud...

Except it's sunny!

62.

What time did dad go to the dentist?

Tooth hurt-y

63.

Waiter: How do you like your eggs?

Dad: I don't know, you haven't brought them out yet.

64.

Waiter: How did you find the food?

Dad: I just looked down, and there it was on my plate.

65.

Did you hear about the guy who can't turn left?

He's alright.

66.

Hey Dad, can February March?

No, but April May.

67.
Can cardboard box?

*No, but
aluminum can!*

68.
**Dad: Did you know that no one
living within 15 miles of that
cemetery are buried there?**

Kid: How come?

Dad: Because they're still alive.

69.
Why did Dad buy a universal remote.

Because it changes everything.

70.
Dad: This milk is from Mexico.

Kid: It is?

Yeah, it says, "Soy milk."

71.
Dad: That ant is a girl.

Kid: How do you know?

Dad: Because if it was a boy it would be called an uncle.

72.
**Who oversees
all the tissues?**

The Handker-Chief.

73.

Why do the scissors never have a jogging partner?

Because you shouldn't run with scissors.

74.

What do you call a pharmacist that helps everyone?

Piller of the community.

75.
Why did the golfer patch his pants?

Because he got a hole in 1.

76.
Where in the house should you store your liquor?

In the alcohall.

77.

Why should you never run in front of or behind a moving car?

If you run in front you'll get tired, if you run behind you'll get exhausted.

78.

How do you make a cheese board?

Tell it boring stories!

79.

What's great
about brewing eucalyptus?

It's high koala-tea!

80.

What is the worst part
of a money addiction?

Withdrawal.

81.
Politics are ridiculous, but do you know what's truly backwards?

Ylurt.

82.
I kicked the tires on the rental car...

I couldn't Budget.
Now it Hertz!

83.

What happens when smog lifts in Southern California?

UCLA

84.

What kind of underwear did Muhammed Ali wear?

Boxers.

85.

I'll tell you about a magic trick that will turn me into a pai of underpants ...

I'll be brief.

86.

Why did Mrs. Clause buy a lot of spices?

Because Santa was cumin to town!

87.

Why is there water all over the bottom of the vegetable crisper?

There's a leek in it.

88.

Why was the corner table at the restaurant so quiet?

Because it was reserved.

89.

Why could you go to jail for making the national bird sick?

Because it's ill eagle.

90.

Dad: I'm leaving you oxygen in my will.

Why?

Dad: Because you're my heir.

91.

Why was the Kleenex® such a great dancer?

Blame it on the boogie!

92.

Why is it unnecessary to open the jam container?

Because it's already a jar.

93.

Did you hear about the comedian cow?

His jokes are cheesy.

94.

Dad, I spilled coffee on my teacher.

That's grounds for suspension.

95.
Knock knock.!!

a.   *Who's there?*
b.   **Who.**
c.   *Who who?*
d.   **You sound like an owl.**

96.
Why was the strawberry late?

He was caught in a jam.

97.

Our friends served electric eel for dinner...

I was shocked.

98.

What's a dog's favorite breakfast?

Woofles.

99.
**Why did the Easter Bunny
study all night?**

He had to take an eggzam.

100.
**What's an original
way catch a rabbit?**

Unique up on it.

Manufactured by Amazon.ca
Bolton, ON

26487589R00028